W9-AGU-269

# THE UNDERWATER WORLD OF SHARKS™

# the GREAT WHITE shark

James Hirsch

The Rosen Publishing Group's
PowerKids Press™
New York

Published in 2001 by The Rosen Publishing Group, Inc.
29 East 21st Street, New York, NY 10010

First Edition

Book Design:  Maria E. Melendez

Photo Credits:  Cover and title page, pp. 4, 5, 8, 9, 11, 12, 13, 16, 19, 20, 21 © Corbis-Bettman; pp. 2, 3, 17 © Animals, Animals; p. 17 © Peter Arnold; pp. 14, 15 © Carl Roessler/Sea Images, Inc.; pp. 1, 4, 6, 7, 11, 12 © Digital Stock CD.

Library of Congress Cataloging-in-Publication Data

Hirsch, James
    The great white shark/ by James Hirsch.
        p. cm.—(The underwater world of sharks)
    Includes index.
    Summary: Introduces the physical characteristics, behavior, and life cycle of the great white shark.
    ISBN 0-8239-5583-4 (lib. bdg. : alk. paper)
    1. White shark—Juvenile literature. [1. White shark. 2. Sharks.] I. Title. II. Series.

    QL638.95.L3 D54  2000
    597.3'3—dc21                                    99-049767

Manufactured in the United States of America

# Contents

# The GREAT WHITE

The great white shark is the biggest meat-eating fish in the world. Its scientific name is *Carcharodon carcharias*. The great white shark has a huge, pointy **snout**. The snout leads the way as the shark looks for **prey** with its small, black eyes. It has eight fins to guide it through the water. When the great white attacks, it opens its giant mouth, showing razor-sharp teeth. Like all fish, the great white's skin is covered with scales for protection. These rough, tiny, teethlike scales are called **denticles**. Denticles feel like sandpaper.

The great white looks scary to humans because it is so large. Some great white sharks grow as long as 21 feet (6.4 m) and weigh up to 7,000 pounds (3,175 kg)!

◄ *Like other sharks, the great white can smell prey up to a quarter of a mile (.4 km) away.*

5

# PREDATOR of the SEA

Great white sharks are **predators**. This means they hunt other creatures in the ocean. Great white sharks are at the top of the animal **food chain**. They eat smaller or weaker animals, but there aren't any animals that eat them. The food chain is nature's way of controlling the size of the animal **population**.

The great white has a dark back and a white belly. The darker color on its back blends with the color of the ocean water. It is hard for other animals to spot the shark in the water. This makes it easier for the shark to attack its prey without warning.

*The great white sneaks up on prey like these sea lions and attacks them without warning.* ▶

# STRONG Jaws, SHARP Teeth

The great white shark has thousands of large teeth. Your teeth are square or round at the edges. A shark's teeth are pointy and **jagged** like a saw. The great white can have up to 20 rows of teeth in its mouth. If a shark loses a tooth, there is always another tooth waiting in the shark's jaw, ready to move into place. A shark might lose and replace 30,000 teeth during its lifetime.

The great white uses its powerful jaw to grab its prey. Lower teeth are used to hold prey. Upper teeth are used to bite prey.

◀ *The picture on the top left shows the tooth of a prehistoric shark called a meglodon. On the bottom is a great white's tooth.*

# At HOME in the SEA

The great white shark likes warm, mild water. It lives so deep in the ocean that humans cannot reach it without special equipment. People usually see great whites when the sharks come to the surface of the water to feed. A great white shark's favorite foods include sea lions and seals.

Sometimes you can spot a great white near the **breeding grounds** of seals and sea lions. Breeding grounds are places where animals live and have babies. Some breeding grounds of seals and sea lions are found off the coasts of the United States, Canada, Australia, and South Africa.

*The great white shark hunts elephant seals, harbor seals, and sea lions off the coast of California.* ▶

# FEEDING Time

The great white gets the energy it needs from eating animals that have a lot of fatty **tissue**. This tissue is called **blubber**. Elephant seals, sea lions, and whales all have a lot of blubber. If a great white takes a bite of an animal without much blubber, like an otter, it might spit it out! The great white is picky about the food it eats.

The great white also eats smaller sharks, fish, and even trash. Sharks have been known to swallow other animals whole. Scientists have opened up the stomach of a dead great white and found a whole four-foot (1.2–m) shark!

◀ *The great white likes to eat animals that have a lot of fat on their bodies.*

The great white shark spends most of its time out of sight. This makes it hard to study this shark except when it feeds. Not much is known about how sharks **mate**. We do know that female sharks hold their eggs inside their bodies until they are ready to give birth. The mother shark holds eggs inside her body for one to two years. Seven to nine sharks can be born at one time. Baby sharks, called pups, are born fully developed. They even have their adult teeth!

After a great white is born, it is left by the mother to take care of itself.

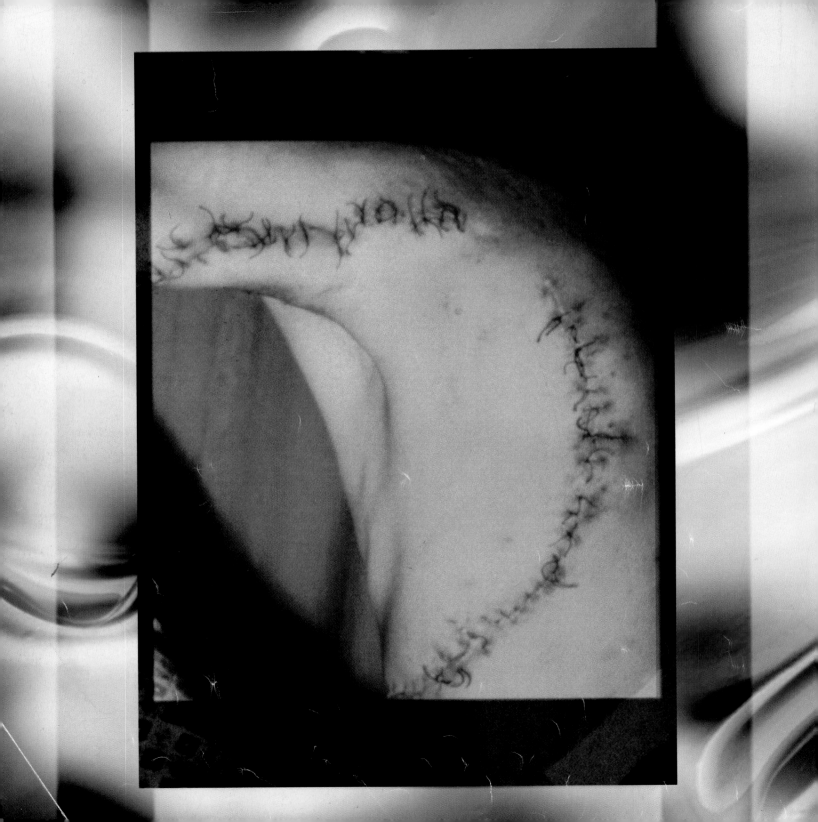

# Shark ATTACKS

The great white shark does not hunt people for food, but sometimes it does attack them. Most attacks happen when a swimmer plays in water near breeding grounds of a shark's prey. A shark can mistake a person for its prey. In some swimming areas, giant nets have been set up in the water to keep sharks from swimming too close to the shore.

Great white sharks don't attack many humans. There are only a few attacks on humans each year. Most of these attacks are not deadly. It is safe to swim in the ocean, just stay away from places where sharks are known to feed.

◀ *A shark attack can leave a big scar on a person's body.*

# Do SHARKS Have ENEMIES?

The greatest enemy a great white shark has is humans. People hunt sharks. They eat shark meat, make necklaces from shark teeth, and use sharkskin to make boots. Hunters have killed so many great white sharks that the **species** is in danger.

Instead of killing sharks, scientists catch them and attach a tag to their fins. Then they return the sharks to the water. The tag helps scientists record the movement of the sharks in the ocean. By doing this, scientists can learn more about the **habits** of the great white shark.

*Hunters were killing so many sharks that we had to pass laws to protect them.* ▶

HEALTHY FOOD
FOR MIDDLE & HIGH AGE PEOPLE

スクアレン スーパー ゴールド
深海鮫エキス

SQUALENE
Super Gold

maruman

村 山

# PROTECTING the Great White Shark

It takes a long time for the shark population to grow. This is because mother sharks **reproduce** only a few times in their lives.

In the early 1990s, South Africa **declared** the great white shark an **endangered species**. Hunters were killing so many sharks that scientists were afraid there would be none left. Other countries have joined the fight to protect great white sharks.

Great white sharks are an important part of ocean life. Instead of killing great white sharks, we need to learn to appreciate their power and beauty.

◄ *We have to protect the great white so the species does not die out.*

21

# Did You KNOW?

- The great white can swim about 15 miles (24.1 km) per hour.
- A great white shark can **breach** like a whale. That means it can leap out of the water!
- In the last 100 years, more people in the United States have died from dog bites than shark bites.
- The great white shark is part of the **mackerel shark** family.
- A great white shark can smell one drop of blood in thousands of gallons (liters) of water.
- A great white shark can live up to 100 years.

# Glossary

**blubber** (BLUH-ber)  The fat of a whale, penguin, or other sea animal.

**breach** (BREECH)  To leap out of the water.

**breeding grounds** (BREED-ing GROWNDZ)  Places where male and female animals come together to have babies.

*Carcharodon carcharias* (kar-CHAR-o-don kar-CHAR-ee-us) The scientific name of the great white shark.

**declared** (dih-KLAHRD)  When something has been announced.

**denticles** (DEN-tuh-kulz)  The tiny teethlike scales on a shark's skin.

**endangered species** (en-DAYN-jerd SPEE-sheez)  A group of living things that is in danger of no longer existing.

**food chain** (FOOD CHAYN)  Living things that are connected because each uses another as food.

**habits** (HA-bitz)  The way something or someone usually behaves.

**jagged** (JAG-ed)  Sharp and uneven.

**mackerel shark** (MA-kuh-ruhl SHARK)  Any member of a family of large sharks that live in deep ocean waters.

**mate** (MAYT)  To join together in order to have babies.

**population** (pop-yoo-LAY-shun)  The number of living things that live in a single place.

**predators** (PREH-duh-terz)  Animals that kill other animals for food.

**prey** (PRAY)  An animal that is hunted by another animal for food.

**reproduce** (ree-pruh-DOOS)  To have babies.

**snout** (SNOWT)  A long nose.

**species** (SPEE-sheez)  A group of living things.

**tissue** (TIH-shoo)  Elements that form parts of living things.

# Index

# Web Sites

To learn more about great white sharks, check out these Web sites:
http:/www.ops.org/boyd/ocean/whshark.htm
http://www.seaworld.org/animal_bytes/greatwhite.ab.html